UP FROM RELIGION

A POETIC MEMOIR

Maurice Lindsay

UP FROM RELIGION

Copyright © 2019 by Maurice Lindsay

All rights reserved. No part of this book may be reproduced or transmitted in any form or by any means, graphic, electronic, or mechanical, including photocopying, recording, taping or by any information storage retrieval system without the written permission of the publisher, except in the case of brief quotations embodied in critical articles and reviews. For more information or inquires in regards to this book, visit AfrovisionsMedia.com.

This publication is for educational purposes only and contains the opinions and ideas of its author. It is sold with the understanding that neither the author nor the publisher is engaged in rendering psychological, mental, legal, financial, or professional advice and services. Readers are encouraged to seek the counsel of competent professionals concerning such matters mentioned above.

4th Print Edition, 2024

Book cover designed by *Danni John.*

PRINT ISBN: 978-1-7328993-9-1

Printed in the *United States of America.*

To my fellow brothers and sisters of African or indigenous descent, I hope my words inspire you to rise above any inherited belief system that is blocking you from becoming your best self!

Contents

Introduction vii

Chapter One: the journey 1

Chapter Two: the healing 45

Chapter Three: the re-education 81

Chapter Four: the lessons 121

Chapter Five: the affirmations 137

Index 153

Acknowledgements 155

About The Author 157

INTRODUCTION

Peace and blessings manifest with every lesson learned. If your knowledge were your wealth then it would be well earned. – Erykah Badu

In 2011, I embarked on a journey of self-discovery that led me down the religious paths of Christianity and the Hebrew Israelite faith. And for the past 7 plus years, I've dedicated my entire life to practicing the teachings within the bible and trying to convert other African-Americans to my religion. I started off as a Christian blogger and then later became a writer and teacher within the Hebrew Israelite movement. I wrote a best-selling book on the identity of the biblical Israelites and ran a top blog about the faith for over 4 years; which had thousands of readers and subscribers from all across the globe.

At the height of my involvement with the movement, as I was in the process of writing my next book on the subject, a series of events happened in my life that caused me to question my belief in both religion and the bible. As a self-taught historian and go-to guy for knowledge on the bible and the Hebrew Israelite faith, I thought I knew everything there was to know about these subjects. But during this time frame, I was exposed to things that I never knew before; things that were there all along but beyond my consciousness.

After these events, I began to study and research daily to verify whether or not my faith was based on facts or fiction. I also began to analyze and re-evaluate my life to see if my religion had made me better or if it had stunted my growth. In the end, I came to the conclusion that my religion and the bible were based on ancient myths and that although its doctrines were beneficial to me in the past, they had also kept me in a box that prevented me from growing.

I'm a truth seeker by nature. So when I realized that what I believed in was a lie, there was no way that I could practice my religion or live by the bible any longer. But this decision was very devastating to me because I had believed in this book for so long and built my entire life around it. Plus I had so many people who followed my teachings and writings, that it made me feel like I had led people astray, which is the last thing I ever wanted to do.

During this process of me rising above my religion, I experienced many growing pains. Because of this, I felt the need to write, as writing is a form of creative expression for me. So one day I decided to write about what I was going through to release the thoughts from my head onto paper. But when I sat down at the table and began typing on my laptop, one of the strangest things happened... poetry came out!

I say strange because I had never written poetry before. I was a historian and blogger and for the last 7 or 8 years of my life, the only form of writing I've done has been articles and essays; except for my personal quotes that I would post online. So when I began writing to express my thoughts on leaving my faith; I was intending to write an article or something. But by the time I noticed, I had written my first poem.

As I continued to write, more poetry came out. Although writing poetry was new to me, I enjoyed it much more than writing articles. Not only did poetry give me a new form of creative expression, but it also became a form of therapy for me. Each week, I wrote new poems expressing my thoughts about the journey I was on; and each week I felt more empowered. After a few months, I had a collection of poetry that tells my story of coming up from religion.

Although this book is about me, like all of my writings, the core purpose of this book is to inspire my people to decolonize our minds from European concepts so that we can become the best version of ourselves. With that being said, I hope this book creates an authentic dialogue on

Western Religion's stronghold on Black America and sets those free who feel bound to religion. Lastly, I hope this book provides answers to those who questioned why I left the faith; and redeems me from any unfair criticism or judgments I've received from doing so.

CHAPTER ONE

....

the journey

church boy

i was born and raised a christian
so the bible was all i knew.
i spent my childhood in the church
learning about god behind the pew.
i heard thousands of sermons
from different pastors we went to.
i couldn't understand what they were saying
but i was taught that it was true.

i used to ask lots of questions
to my mom and people that i knew.
but the answers seemed irrelevant
to what black people were going through.
so i lost interest in the church early
and only went cuz i had to.

this caused me to act out in rebellion
which my mom called a bad attitude
she was probably right tho
but i didn't mean to be rude
i just didn't like to be forced to go,
i wanted the option to choose.

UP FROM RELIGION

but when i asked to stay home,
they always refused.
mamma didn't play dat,
it was their house, so there rules.
i didn't understand that back then tho,
so i grew up angry and confused.
and when i became of age
i left their house and the pews.

dope boy

dissatisfied with the church,
i surrendered to my environment.
most of the older homies were hustlers
so i became a dope boy scientist.

i spent most of my younger days
just tryna get paid.
trapping out my 93 buick
selling weed and yay.

me and my homie b.j. would hit the strip clubs
in south charlotte and sell the strippers coke.
then i would drive back to columbia and
flood the streets with california kush to smoke.

and when the streets got too hot
to hustle around my way.
i would spend a month or two
in the burg with my old boo, ebby j.
turning her apartment into a trap house
while she went to work during the day.
being broke was obsolete,
i was bout getting money any and every way.
but i knew it was only temporary so
i was always searching for a better way.

UP FROM RELIGION

then my homie jeremy got murdered
by my old roommate's brother.
the year after that, my homie BJ got busted for
selling dope to an undercover.

we were together every day
so i could have received the same fate.
not wanting to end up like them
i decided to leave 704 and move back to the 80-tre.

vulnerable and open to change, i took a
job during the day and reduced my hustling to nights.
to keep the police off my back while i decided
on what i wanted to do with my life.

searching for answers,
i began reading books.
and for the first time since my youth,
something other than money, sex, or sports had me hooked.

i fell in love with reading
and the knowledge that i was gaining.
it allowed me to see that i could be whatever
i wanted if my mind wasn't so tainted.

so i decided to return back to church
and leave the streets alone.
i gave my life to christ
in an effort to right my wrongs.

back 2 church

after 7 years of sinning,
i desired to change my life.
i was tired of how i was living
and wanted to end the strife.
then one day i met a fine young lady
who would later become my wife.
that went to church every sunday
and re-introduced me to the christian life.

since all i knew was this religion,
i ended up going back to the church.
they preached that jesus was the only way,
and i wanted to see him work.
so i gave my life to the lord
and let go of my worldly perks.
became a student of the bible,
seeking to quench my inner thirst.

then one day my lady brought
some things to my attention.
about how what the pastor preached
was so much different than what was written.
so i looked into this matter
and later noticed that she wasn't kidding.
what was happening in the church versus

what was in the bible seemed like a total contradiction.
pastors were twisting scriptures up
talking about god giving them a vision,
just to increase the tithes and offerings,
so they could attain their financial ambitions.
of living in big houses and driving mercedes-benzes
while church folk struggling, facing evictions.

so we ended up leaving this church
after i started peeping game.
we visited other churches
but found much to be the same.
instead of giving people solutions,
they taught 'em how to endure pain.
promising people blessings for obedience
that never ever came.
looking back on these teachings,
they were purely insane.
making people choose faith,
over using their brain.
so i woke up and
took off those mental chains,
and made a conscious decision
to never go back 2 church again.

locked up by religion

i ran away from the streets
to dodge prison and the police
and jumped straight into religion
only to end up locked into a prison
of someone else's beliefs.

in the beginning, it gave me peace,
but over time as my knowledge increased,
i realized that my faith was blocking
me from the real truth that i'd seek
only allowing me to go so far
like a dog on a leash.

worse than that, it was also
making me judgmental as can be.
only had the eyes to see the flaws
of others but blinded at the ones within me.
i never thought that religion
could do this to me.

i went from selling weed
and coke to my own peeps
to judging folks over how many

commandments they keep
thinking i'm woke cuz i had knowledge
but everyone else was sleep.

my faith was
making me weak.
like a bodybuilder
with no physique
causing me to forget to
practice what i preached.
and all of the g codes that
i learned from the streets.

looking in the mirror
and no longer liking what i see.
i decided that the torah and the bible
were no longer good for me.
so i took off the chains round my brain
using knowledge as my key.
and i broke out of this religion
so that i could be free.

i thought we were israelites

i wrote the book on how to wake up to your true identity
only to find out that i haven't even awakened to *mines*.
i thought i was a hebrew israelite
due to the biblical *signs*.
running parallel to our people's
oppression in our modern-day *times*.
plus i did the research
on many african *tribes*
who stated that they are descendants
of those biblical israelite *tribes*.
and since many of our ancestors
came from those same african *tribes*,
it seemed pretty accurate that
we were the biblical *tribes*.

this gave me the confidence to write a book *about it*
teaching my people *about it*
which led me to reach people all over the world
asking me questions *about it*.
so i began to write articles on my website *about it*.
some went viral and people began to talk *about it*.
then suddenly, i became a historian *about it*.

i didn't plan this, so i thought it was a *sign*.
that i was the man for this, called by the *divine*.
so i wrote more content about us
being the people of *zion*.
i believed in it 100% so i was bold as a *lion*.
i took my message to radio stations
and even did a book *signing*.
and when people heard my message
they thought it was *inspiring*.
then my ego got big
without me even *trying*.
i thought i knew everything,
if I said it, then there was no *denying*.

but as years went on,
and i began learning more *history*
i discovered things about the bible
that to me was a *mystery*.
like when i read the original versions of the gospels
that were hidden away from *publicity*.
or when i found evidence of the biblical stories
being plagiarized from egyptian *antiquity*.
i thought i was a great researcher so
i couldn't believe all these things were *hidden from me*
finding out everything i believed in was a lie

can you imagine what this *did to me*?
at first, i was depressed,
which caused me to humble myself *instantly*.
then i went back to the drawing board of
what i thought was my true *identity*.

torah blues

what started off as good
turned bad after some years.
i went from making people better
to making people shed tears.

my dedication to the torah
turned me into a pharisee.
instead of the good in people,
i could only see the sin in thee.
i cut family and friends off who
i deemed to be living unrighteously.
as if i was the standard
and had no flaws within me.

i followed leaders and teachers
that made women the lesser and men the larger.
and i started adopting their ways; treating my wife
like my slave instead of my partner.

the torah became my god
whatever it said, i did it.
i taught it to my daughters;
and whatever they asked to do, i'd forbid it.

UP FROM RELIGION

i thought i was living right
but my life seemed so wrong.
everyone that i loved,
we seemed to not just get along.

on the surface, i kept it going
but in my mind, i often felt insane.
i just didn't understand how my faith
would end up causing me so much pain.

what was happening to my life
or better yet; what was happening to me?
i was the main cause of my family's dysfunction
yet i was too blinded by the torah to see.

torah gave me discipline
but it also gave me blues.
i lost my ability to think for myself
and became a slave to written rules.

following the followers

everybody claims to be teachers
everybody claims to be a prophet.
fronting like they met god face to face
and he gave them all his knowledge.
as if they hadn't read many books
or learned the scripts from a seminary college.
yet they speak as if they're moses
like they every word is solid.

new youtube preachers popping up
every day left and right.
and everybody flocking to them
looking for some light.
to bring us out of the dark darkness
of our 400 year plight.
and free us from our sins
so we can finally live right.

i was one of the many
following these preachers too.
i discovered i was a hebrew israelite
from the docs and lessons on the tube.
but i was too wise to follow strangers

so i reached out to some of these dudes.
i spoke with various elders and
they gave me their take on the good news.
i heard all kinds of different
perspectives and angles on the faith.
some called it *the walk*,
and others called it *the way*.
but much like christianity, the leaders were
interpreting the scriptures in their own way.
acting as the leading authority on
what the bible had to say.

this was interesting to me.
cuz many of the leaders were learning about
the faith as they went.
yet when the cameras come on
they would act as if they
were divinely sent.

one ministry we fellowshipped with
was only in the faith for like a year.
yet was preaching about the culture
like they was raised as a seer.

ego seemed to be
behind most of the leaders.
which was funny. cuz i seemed

to know more than most of these leaders.
yet i was deceived like most,
and still followed some of their teachings.
not the ones who i exposed. but the
ones who were practicing what they were preaching.

but after my eyes began to open
and i finally saw the bible for what it was.
i realized that i had been bamboozled.
and that religion is one hell of a drug.

had me and my people addicted
to a book that had been a thousand times rewritten.
and handed down to us by those who
hung us on trees and raped our women.

this drug affects us all so i ain't mad at
none of the leaders that i once followed.
cuz most hebrew israelite preachers and teachers
are just as deceived as those they followed.

this why after all these years of preaching
not a damn thang has changed.
cuz we mentally enslaved to the same
religions that put our ancestors in chains.

so we continue to reap more
oppression, poverty, confusion, and pain.
while we wait on the return of a messiah
that never historically came.

on my own: true story

i gave my life to the faith
and the growth of the movement.
i devoted every single day to my studies
and the betterment of my students.

i wasn't in it for fame
i was in it for soul salvation.
and i was dedicated 100% to
rebuilding the hebrew nation.

…..

all the elders and teachers kept
talking about preparing for the fall of
babylon and the return of the messiah.
and that we need to move off the grid
so we could keep the commandments
and rid our flesh of evil desires.

some taught that we should stay in
america and prepare for babylon's fall here
others said that we should move to africa
where we would be treated more fair.

UP FROM RELIGION

these messages resonated with me
cuz the hebrews lived this way as well.
so i took it to heart and me and my wife
put all our possessions up for sale.

we moved our family off the grid
thousands of miles away to the mountains.
and learned how to be self-sufficient
living without the conveniences of modern housing.

i had plans of building a community for other
hebrews who wanted to escape the rat race.
a lot of families showed interest but i found out later
most was just talking out the side of their face.

only one family supported us
all throughout the journey.
and for that, the "hosey's"
will forever be my homies.

·····

plans didn't work out
so after 90 days off the grid we
decided to move back down south.

we had to tie up some loose ends back home
and figure out our next location before moving back out.

money was getting low
and we needed a place to stay.
so i purchased some land
and a travel trailer for us
to live in. outside the city. far away.

the deal turned out to be bogus tho and
the owner refused to give me my money back.
i was superheated so i devised a plan to go to his krib and
shoot em dead to get my money back.

but my wife talked me out of it
telling me about the kids and not wanting
to visit me in prison.
and that i needed to depend on *yah*
for all of my provisions.
i was hesitant at first,
but in the end, i decided to listen.
so we ended up living
in our car with my 2 children.

…..

embarrassed, pissed off
, and confused on what to do next.
we prayed to *yah* daily for answers
but he never responded; which kept me vexed.

so we ended up getting a cheap apartment
in the hood to have a roof over our heads.
but for us, it was temporary to stack
up some bread to get ahead.

meanwhile, elders that i followed
were telling folks that *yah* said his people
need to leave america and
move to africa before destruction.
plus some hebrews that we knew
who moved to africa from america
were giving us the same instructions.

there was a feeling in the air
nationwide among hebrews that america
was about to fall.
and that we needed to
follow Jerimiah 51 and flee Babylon
before the last trumpet called.

i never felt home in america anyway,
so we decided to move to africa
and never come back.
but we didn't have the money
for the plane tickets and all that.

so a friend of my wife living in africa
influenced us to start a go fund me
campaign to raise money for us to move out.
i didn't want to do it but i was
out of options and i felt
my followers would look out.

her and husband told us to have faith
and that *yah* would make a way.
so we broke our apartment lease
and rented a room at an extended stay.

…..

we thought the campaign
would work but it turned out to be a disaster.
after 3 months of promotions,
we couldn't even afford to buy one ticket;
so our plans were shattered.

i couldn't believe that the
people i gave my all to
didn't return the favor.
out of 1800 followers,
only 12 people
donated to aid us.

the family in africa
donated the most.
they did all they could
to get us to africa but
no one else came close.

money ran low and we
could no longer afford the hotel rent.
so we were forced to move in
with my parents which had me bent.

"where the hell are you at *yah*?
for once, show yo face.
for you, i kept the faith. i even gave up my own place.
the least you can do is provide me somewhere to stay."

he replied back to me with
silence as he always does.

which caused me to lose faith in him
cuz he was no longer worthy of my trust.

so i let god go and started
making things happen on my own.
without the sabbath as a burden,
i was able to work my ass off for 30 days straight
and put us in a beautiful home.

no help from above,
i did it all ground zero.
had to go back to hustle mentality
and become my own hero.

and for the first time
in a long time we
finally began to win.
my wife was happy.
my lil ones was happy.
and i knew i was
the only one on whom
i could depend.

…..

UP FROM RELIGION

i made a PSA to my followers
that i was done with the HBI movement.
and now embracing indigenous pan-africanism
as my new ideology for our people's improvement.

most people were shocked
and disappointed by my decision.
but a few rocked with me and
chose truth over tradition.

up from religion

religion is a prison
that i spent the last 7 years locked in.
i started off a christian
then converted to the hebrew israelite doctrine.

in the beginning, it was good,
it gave me structure and discipline.
but over time it became bondage,
just too many restrictions.

however, i kept on following
cuz i truly believed in this religion.
it was the only belief system
that explained our people's condition.

according to deuteronomy 28, verses 15 through 68,
god sent us in slavery for disobeying his commissions.
and that we needed to return back to his laws
for him to relinquish his decision.

so i kept all of his laws
for years with precision,
believing that one day he would come and
save us from the opposition.

but as time passed,
i began to feel like i was in prison.
i felt like anything i did
i had to ask god for permission.

scared to lose salvation
and miss our future redemption,
i was bound by a book
that kept me in indecision.
so i began to ask questions
and research this religion.
not only the hebrew israelites,
but all bible-based religions.

come to find out,
they're all based on superstitions…
at least 70% of the bible is plagiarized
from the writings of ancient egyptians.

discovering this truth,
freed me from religion.
now i can breathe again,
and make my own decisions.

ode to moms & pops

i never seen a love
like y'all's before.
you've done so much for me
i can't even keep the score.

moms been my rock
ever since joey left the mix.
pops been raising me as his own
since i was like five or six.

y'all gave me a wonderful childhood
despite our financial struggles.
you always encouraged my dreams
despite me always being in trouble.

moms taught me the bible
and kept me in the church.
pops gave me discipline
and showed me how to work.

your morals were a blessing
but for my life i want something different.
you raised me in the hood
so getting money was my interest.

UP FROM RELIGION

i wanted to pay you back
for all the good you done for me.
but i got caught up in the streets
flipping quarter pounds of weed.

i don't know how you put up with me
i gave you two so much hell.
but you always showed me love
pops even bailed me out of jail.

looking to get my life together
i returned back to what you taught me.
i became a christian again and started
changing before death caught me.

but after some years
i left the church to follow the torah.
mama didn't say she was hurt,
but i could see it in her aura.

once i left christianity
for the hebrew israelites
our relationship took some
quick downward spikes.

i was so passionate about my beliefs
that i condemned you over yours.
had some overly heated debates with moms
that caused some family wars.

i distanced myself from you and the family
because i thought you were pagans.
according to the hebrew israelites doctrine
christianity was of satan.

then a change of events happened
that caused me to hit rock-bottom.
i needed a place to stay and y'all
welcomed my family in with solemn.

the same house i grew up in,
i ended up moving right back in.
and despite all our differences, you were
there to help me get back on my feet again.

while staying at yo krib,
something inside led me to research the origins of religion.
and i found out that the bible was plagiarized
from the ancient sumerians and egyptians.

this discovery caused me a lot of pain
but it made a lot of sense.
i can't believe i allowed a man-made book
to keep us divided like a fence.

i'm sorry for all of the pain that our
differences in religion have caused you.
i love you both to death and i just
wanted to thank and applaud you.

salute to wifey

sweet as honey,
kind, and genuine.
beautifully dripped in
mahogany melanin.

her presence so elegant.
her convo so relevant.
everything about her
seemed just so heaven-sent.

like a queen in a palace,
she commanded my attention.
her laughter and good vibes
drew me in from the beginning.

she was a breath of fresh air
from the life i was living.
so spending time with her
made me feel like i was winning.

she changed my world;
made life seem more appealing.
she even reintroduced me to
the concept of religion.

UP FROM RELIGION

she was mad loyal and
supported everything i was building.
so i decided to marry her
and take in her 3 children.

we began our new life together
like d'angelo, just cruising.
then we became hebrew israelites
and things got very confusing.

we had our ups and down
and did a lot of moving.
but she always held me down
even tho dudes was choosing.

i wanted to give her the world
but our religion kept us in seclusion.
so she just made the best of it
in spite of our conclusion.

she stuck by my side
throughout all of the confusion.
she even trusted my leadership
out of our religious delusion.

now that we're awake
and no longer snoozing.
i plan to give her a life
that's much more amusing.

like an egyptian lotus flower,
i just wanna see her blooming.
she is my queen and the only woman
i wanna spend my life pursuing.

forgive me queens

my wife blessed me
with 4 beautiful girls.
3 not from my seed, but still
very much a part of my world.

never been a dad,
so raising 4 queens is no easy task.
not having a blueprint,
i use religion as my mask.

i thought the torah was the truth
so i taught it to my youth.
they never was really feelin it
but i didn't accept their excuse.

i forbade them from foolery
and worldly activities.
we only allowed them to
participate in hebrew festivities.

i tried to make things fun for
kay, bree, mariah, and lauren.
but to them everything we did
just seemed to be boring.

as the years passed,
i became stricter and stricter.
so much so that it seemed they no longer
wanted me to be a part of the picture.

we did a lot moving
being led to places of god's choosing.
but little did i know,
it was causing my girl's ruin.

3 ended up leaving us
choosing to live with their dad and grands.
only one daughter remained
who was too young to understand.

adhering to religion
enslaved me to laws of being a black jew.
but little did i know
i was locking my girls up too.

in case i never fully expressed it
i love you kayla, lauren, mariah and bree.
and no matter what happens,
you will always be a part of me.

r.i.p. cliff

i didn't realize
how much you loved me
until you were gone.

we never had a
had a close relationship
we never even spoke on the phone.

but you always been
good to me and you
always kept it real.

you spoke your
mind to everybody
regardless of how they feel.

we spoke more often
before me and your
daughter converted to our religion.

after that, i began
to judge you and look
at you different.

you and ashley
weren't that close
which made her feel some type of way.

but when she found
out you were dying
she wanted to move back right away.

so we moved back to
south carolina so she could
be around you for your last days.

and during this time
all of my pre-judgments
about you began to fade.

one of your last nights
in the hospital, you
told me that you loved me.

i never heard you
say that before so i
reached over and you hugged me.

UP FROM RELIGION

but at the time
i was still religious
so i thought you were going to hell.
then after you died,
i cried my eyes out
and my heart began to swell.

after your death,
my search for truth
outside my religion began.

i figured there was no
way a man like cliff
could have died in sin.

and from my research
i discovered that both
my beliefs and the bible were lies.

i just wish
i had known all of this
before you died.

every 7 years

i spent 7 years in the streets
followed by 7 years of *religion*
and through both phases of my life
i kinda felt like something was *missing*.
like i was meant for something better
or maybe something just *different*.
from selling weed and dope
or teaching my people what was *written*.

i would often have these dreams
of me bettering our people's *condition*.
but i was either baggin grams in the *kitchen*
or converting folks to the hebrew israelite *religion*.
both lives gave me purpose,
one gave me *vision*.
and the other gave me *discipline*.
but they both prevented me
from fulfilling my life's *mission*.

so after 14 years of *experimentin*
i finally surrendered to my *intuition*
and then one night i had a dream that
told me what to do and i *listened*.

UP FROM RELIGION

at first i hit rock bottom,
which caused me to question my *decision*.
but eventually, i realized that was carrying dead weight
from both lives and needed a new *beginning*.

i needed spiritual *healing*
from my past life of *sinning*
along with the guilt from my *religion*
and spent the next few months on an inner journey
until i realized i had been *forgiven*.

not from a god in the sky
but from the god that lives *within*.
and for the next 7 years, i plan to help others
overcome where i had just *been*.
so that we can put an end to the
post-traumatic slave syndromes of
the future gen-er-*ration*.

CHAPTER TWO

············●●●●●●●············

the healing

biblical oppression

the bible teaches africans that we are
cursed for disobeying god's laws.
yet the europeans seemed to be blessed
for violating those same laws.

they break all of his commandments
and receive tenfold in worldly advancements.
while we steady trying to keep his commandments
but remain under the same oppressive circumstances.

this tells me that white folks are doing
something right and we're doing something wrong.
like believing in a book that's
been misguiding us for so long.

but according to believers,
this is all part of the lord's will.
and to never question god,
regardless of how we feel.

with a mindset like this,
we will never be blessed.
because a book can't free those,
whom it was meant to oppress.

UP FROM RELIGION

the bible may be good for some,
but it oppressed the hell out of me.
therefore i'm leaving it behind
so that i can be free.

the jesus myth

i used to believe in jesus and
that he was coming back to save us.
until i researched history and
discovered that he was used to enslave us.

jesus of loebuck was the name of a slave ship
that brought us here in chains.
it was named after the jesus in the bible,
who promised to redeem the slain.

but this jesus in the bible
never came back to see about us.
even after 400 years of oppression,
he never came back for us.

so i did a background check on jesus
and found that he never really existed.
he was just a myth created by the romans
so christianity could be invented.

at the council of nicea in 325 ad,
jesus the christ first came to be.
he was created by combining the
deities of serapis and krishna into thee.

then they created images of him
so people wouldn't think he's fiction.
cuz round that time there was already
hundreds of gods in existence.

originally the image of Jesus was black,
but in the 15th century, they painted him white.
so that future generations
would think that god was white.

next, they go to Africa
to enslave our ancestors in the name of jesus.
telling them that they were soul-less savages
that were filled with hosts of demons.

they said that we were born sinners
in need of jesus forgiveness.
we couldn't read or speak their languages
so we had no idea the character was fictitious.

then they taught us about his kingdom
and how it was somewhere in the sky.
a place he would come back and take
us to sometime after we die.

our ancestors took on this faith
cuz since like one of their own.
plus it helped them to cope with slavery
being miles away from home.

so although jesus never did anything
for us during our earthly life.
we looked forward to experiencing
him during our afterlife.

this belief was passed down
from generation to generation.
which is why after 400 years later,
we still patiently waiting.

and not too long ago
i used to believe in him too.
but unfortunately,
most of my people still do.

UP FROM RELIGION

god ain't good

if god is so great,
how come he only shows up when it's too late?
how come he allowed us to go into slavery
but let the europeans escape.
and why does he allow bad things to happen
like women getting raped?
and why doesn't he put food
on homeless people's plates?

and don't tell me no mess about
about god gave us free will,
because god got free will too
and instead of using it to heal,
he falls back and watches us get killed.
so either god don't care about how we feel,
or god simply just ain't real.

and based on our last 400 years,
i'm starting to believe the latter.
cuz we the most religious people on the planet,
yet to god, black lives don't seem to matter.

he allows us to get murdered
in his streets as well as his churches.

and we pray for miracles and blessings,
yet only seem to receive curses.

our relationship with god just
don't seem to be working for us.
no matter how much we serve him,
he helps everybody except us.

so i decided to put god to the test
and ask him some questions.
if you are god then show up
for me or stop fronting.
after months of no responses
and a lot of frustration,
i lost faith in god without hesitation.

he did nothing for me
to prove his existence,
so there was no longer a point in
serving a god that is so distant.

one that doesn't answer prayers
or show up when you need him,
yet gets mad at you
when you don't believe in him.

UP FROM RELIGION

a god like this
does not deserve any praise.
and ever since i left him behind,
i've been seeing better days.

self-righteous

i think i was a better person
before i converted to the bible.
yeah, i had a lot of vices
but at least i was reliable.

my peeps and my friends
could always count on me to be there for them.
without judgment or condemnation
cuz i sincerely cared for them.

but after conversion,
my loyalty began shifting.
away from the people that i loved
and closer to my religion.

my beliefs had me tripping,
placing my principles over people.
causing me to view all those
who didn't believe like me as being unequal.

friendships and kinships
suffered as a result.
and i replaced them with
others from my faith, like a cult.

UP FROM RELIGION

trying to follow jesus,
i was willing to cut everybody off.
even the relationships with my parents
got lost in the sauce.

i used to be okay with this,
because it was mentioned in the word.
that you would have to cut people off
who wasn't a part of jesus' herd.

and like a lost sheep,
i believed in it.
devoted my life
a hundred percent to it.

but after years of living like this,
i started disliking the person i had become.
then one day i realized that my religion
made me forget where i come from.

as a child having to warm his
washing water up over the stove,
i never thought i'd grow up and
treat people so cold.

like i said in the beginning,
i was a better person before religion.
so i think it's time to go back
to my humble beginnings.

UP FROM RELIGION

who is god?

i used to believe that
god lived in the sky.
and i was taught that if you prayed to him,
then he would reply
so i spent years and years
praying to the most high.
but i never heard from him,
despite my efforts to try.

then one day somebody told me
that god lived inside of me.
so i stopped looking for a response
from something outside of me.
i looked within myself and
started praying very mindfully.
and then i finally heard this voice
reply back to me silently.

nobody heard it but me,
cuz it came from within.
at first, i thought i was tripping,
until it spoke to me again.
it told me what to do about
a sticky situation i was in.

so i followed the instructions
and came out with a win.

i didn't know whose voice it was,
but i knew it wasn't me,
so i just accredited it to god
cuz I didn't know who else it could be
but later i learned that this voice
did not come from a deity,
it came from the spirit of the universe
that lives within me.

some people give it names
but i call it the great spirit.
it always lived within me,
but i was programmed to fear it.

but now that i'm up from religion,
i can finally hear it.
and whenever it speaks,
it's always quiet, but coherent.

this is god to me.
and it's not a he or she.
it's the supreme spirit of the universe
manifesting through me.

lost is the way

after leaving the faith,
i became a little lost.
i didn't know where i was going,
because *yah* was no longer my boss.

free to find my own way,
i began searching different paths.
found some that resonated with me
and others that just made me laugh.

the journey was enlightening and
heartbreaking at the same time.
cuz i discovered that what i once
believed had me walking round blind.

from being able to see the truth that
was hidden in plain sight.
that i had everything i needed living within me
in order to make my life right.

which led me to the revelation that
i was the god that i was searching for all along.
and that i just needed to lose my religion
to find my way back home.

revelations

i been reading the bible since a youth
but the man upstairs never came through.

i went from being a christian to a brew
til i found out they both wasn't true.

got tired of looking in the bible for a play
i decided to go my own way.

no mo living by a book that's leading
me and my people the wrong way.

religion ain't help nobody,
all it did was enslave our bodies.

trying to save the soul of everybody
is really just a tool to control everybody.

i learned the truth for myself
so can't nobody tell me anything else.

if you looking for god, look in yourself
cuz you won't find'em anywhere else.

my way out

i was in so deep,
i couldn't see my way out.
drowning in doctrines & prophecies
that never seemed to play out.
in need of some fresh air,
i started researching things out.
which led me to discover
what the bible was really all about.
that it was all man-made
based on other ancient historical accounts.
then taught to us as truth
to keep mentally enslaved with no clout.
then i saw the truth and it gave me
the strength to come out.
so i placed my head above water
and my ancestors reached out.
they guided me towards the truth
and helped me to throw the lies out.
now i'm free to live on purpose
because i found my way out.

humbled

i thought i knew everything
until i found out that i knew nothing.
i thought the bible was the truth
until i found out that it wasn't.
i thought that faith could move mountains
until i found out that it doesn't.
i thought that *yah* was the only god
until i found out he was one of dozens.
i thought that *yahusha* was my savior
until i found out that he was never coming.
i thought that hell was real
until i found out that the church was bluffing.
i thought that i was going to heaven.
until i found out that i was bugging.
i thought that i was living righteous
until i found out about this discussion.

no mo

no mo religion,
i'm now free to look within myself.
no mo pretending,
i'm now free to just be myself.
no mo dismissing,
i'm now free to speak what i had felt.
no mo indecision,
i'm now free from waiting for god's help.

no mo judging others,
i'm now free to just let people be.
no mo self-righteousness,
i'm now free to notice the flaws within me.
no mo believing in myths,
i'm now free to have eyes that can see.
no mo preventing my growth,
i'm now free to sprout up like a tree.

freedom

can't nobody give you freedom.
either you free or you ain't.

free to be yourself.
whether that's a thug or a saint.

free to live your life.
while you explore what's wrong and right.

free to change and grow
as you reap what you sow.

free to choose a god
instead of being forced to believe in one against all the odds.

free to think for yourself,
without always being influenced by someone else.

free to live off our own land and control it
instead of being ruled by those who stole it.

free to explore nature
and not be condemned by those who hate her.
free to call on your ancestors,
without being labeled by religious protesters.

UP FROM RELIGION

free to say i don't believe in christ
when people try to convert you to the christian life.

free to live by universal laws,
instead of being bound to a book of flaws.

free to not be labeled an atheist
just because i believe the bible was written by plagiarists.

free to promote black empowerment to my people
and not be called a racist by those who treat us unequal.

free to disagree with relationships that go against nature
without being called a homophobic or a hater.

free to express myself authentic-ally
without worrying about who gets offended by me.

but can't nobody give me freedom.
either I am or I ain't.

free to be myself,
regardless of what other people thank.

kush therapy

shortly after finding out
that the bible wasn't a 100.
i found mary jane and
went back to getting blunted.

trying to calm my nerves
puffing l's in the dark of night
meditating on all the years
i wasted believing in christ.

the smell of mangos
coming through the ashes of my rolling papers
conquering my demons
that entered me from reading them bible papers.

smoking with spiritual intentions
just like the ancients did it.
gave me clarity of my visions
removing the self-righteousness that hid it.

coming full circle with the
actions i used to condemn
removed my ability to point the finger
and say that I wasn't him.

UP FROM RELIGION

free to see with new eyes
helped me to re-a-lize
that i'm no better than my brothas
still on the corner getting high or flipping pies.

felt so good to be free
i became addicted to weed again.
not feeling like myself
until i burned some trees again.

one joint turned to 10
and 10 turned to 40,
so after my nights in the wilderness
i decided to quit mary j and end our journey.

but i appreciated the lessons
that she taught me in the clouds
now that i'm back down to earth
they say i'm much more profound.

tho i don't smoke no mo,
if need be, i'll light one up again.
cuz i'm a free spirit
no longer bound to sin.

evolution

each year i evolve
so each year i change.
more knowledge brings
more growth, but it also brings pain.

pain from growing apart from
friendships i thought would never end.
pain from visiting my old hoods
and no longer fitting in.

i graduated from trapping
and mastered in religion.
converted thousands to my faith
and then abandoned the same religion.

some think i'm hypocritical
while others think I'm super spiritual.
i'm so misunderstood that sometimes
it makes me feel hysterical.

so i linked up with a spiritualist
who was a former hebrew israelite.
and she gave me an ancestral reading that
gave me some divine insight.

UP FROM RELIGION

she taught me how to reach my ancestors
by combining nature and rituals.
but i kept it to myself because these
practices weren't scriptural.

then i began looking into
indigenous spiritual practices and
that resonated with my frequencies.
i learned how to meditate and
balance out my chakras to get
my mind and body in synchrony.

this helped me snap out of my funk
and appreciate my growth.
realizing that life is a journey and
i've done more evolving than most.

and through each of my transitions,
the gains outweighed the losses.
i inspired many i crossed paths with
to love themselves. their people.
and to become their own bosses.

so forget what he and she
gotta to say about me.
these are my shoes to walk in
and can't nobody fit in 'em but me.

so walk in them, i will
and wherever they take me, i'll go.
i am an old soul who reincarnated
again just to learn and grow.

grow from the lessons
unlearned in my past lifetimes.
so i can graduate from this earth
and experience a new lifeline.

evolution is the key
for me to reach my destiny.
and I'm looking forward to
manifesting the very best of me.

native american roots

i fought so hard
to claim hebrew
that i neglected my
native american roots.
i knew it was in my blood
but i was too indoctrinated
to accept the truth.

my granddad was a
black native indian
along with all of his descendants.
but i was taught not
to accept history that
didn't line up with genesis.

so i dismissed my own
heritage to claim the tribes of the bible.
until i found out years later
that the bible was plagiarized
and therefore not reliable.

the mystery of my roots
caused me to do some digging.
and i came across some info
about black natives that
caucasians kept hidden.

the original black
native americans were
kushites, nubians, and egyptians
from ancient africa.
who migrated all over the globe and
first discovered india, australia, and america.

a sect of them was
from royal priesthoods
and had divine abilities.
the biblical story of the
hebrews is based on
them and their nobility.

but they had no religion,
they just lived according to nature.
practicing the universal laws of Ma'at
allowed them to be their own savior.

they were spiritualists, herbalists
shamans, astrologers, and prophets.
and they lived off the land so they
wasn't concerned with profits.

some called them indigo
which means original.
some called them africans,
which are the same people.

finding this out
made me proud of my heritage.
cuz just like africa,
america is also my inheritance.

for my little ones

you are more than my
children. you are my seed.
the fruit of yo mama's tree
and the branch of me.

when i see you, i smile
cause i see myself in your eyes.
your mannerisms and melanin
remind me of mines.

2 boys, 1 gurl.
all unique, yet the same.
offsprings of the dark-mattered
cosmos from which we all came.

i love you to the moon and back,
from the sun to Jupiter, my ruling planet.
your existence gives me purpose and
i don't take you for granted.

you are born gods,
ain't no need to look for one elsewhere.
i been through those delusions
and they all lead to nowhere.

UP FROM RELIGION

everything you need
already lives inside.
i'm just here to help you
by being your guide.

and as i teach you,
i'm also learning from you.
i would not be who i am today
if it wasn't for you.

i hope these words
express my love and vibe.
thanks mariah, lamad, and omari
for being born into my tribe.

ode to malcolm

malcom x is my hero
he's the messiah to me.
he resurrected my consciousness
and gave me eyes to see.

how america's systematic oppression
prevented my people's progression
and many other things i never learned
in my history lessons.

malcolm was ahead of his time
and changed so many lives besides mines.
he loved his people so much
that he put his life on the line.

fighting for the black liberation
of future generations.
gives me the obligation
to pick up his torch until we see the manifestation.

tho i disagree with his religion,
i respect his decision.
to choose a god that he felt
would help him fulfill his life's mission.

UP FROM RELIGION

religion deceives us all
and malcom x was no exception.
but to me he was still the greatest
black leader we've had, without question.

purpose

i never desired to be a leader
i only desired to make a difference.
but it was prophesied when i was young
that my words would travel distance.

the ancestors told this to my mom
tho she said it came from the lord.
but regardless of who said it;
i'm the one the message was for.

so i don't take lightly;
the torch that i have been given.
i use my gift to spread truth to
those who will listen

i'm not into titles or accolades
i'm just a servant of my people.
trying to write words that liberate
black minds from feeling unequal.

i thought religion was the way
so for years, i wrote from that perspective.
now i'm free to think for myself;
and i'm much more effective.

UP FROM RELIGION

feels good to be living out the
dreams of my ancestors' prophecies.
now that i'm up from religion;
there ain't nothing stopping me.

CHAPTER THREE

the re-education

mind control

bound by a book
that's based on a lie.
got black people shook
praying to a white man in the sky.

we so scared to go to hell
that we miss out on the now.
we know our lives are miserable,
but religion keeps us in denial.

pastors sell us hope
and we get hooked on it like dope.
givin 'em all our money
which is why we remain broke.

but they tell us to rely
on god to pay our bills
tho they rely on us
to pay their bills

yet we can't give it up,
cuz we bound by church lies
thinking if we stop going,
we'll miss out on a trip to the skies.

UP FROM RELIGION

so we forever remain addicted
to our oppressors' religion.
and we feed it to our children
who grow up making the same decisions.

religion ain't saving us
it's enslaving us.
making us trust in a book
that our oppressors gave to us.

ain't no hell

religion keeps the oppressed
from killing their oppressors.
got 'em too scared to go to hell
to play the role of the aggressor.

but hell never existed,
it was invented by the greeks.
to keep those they conquered
in submission like sheep.

so hell only exists
to those who believe in it.
if you don't want to go to hell
then just stop believing in it.

the real hell is the experience
of black people's existence
being ruled by caucasians
and murdered for resistance.

if you tired of living in hell,
then do something for your people
and strop trying to integrate
with those who treat us unequal.

facts vs. faith

faith and facts
are 2 different things.
facts is based on evidence
and faith is something unseen.

it's like the color of the sky
that we all know is blue.
versus
a man name jesus
who supposedly died for you.

both examples are believed in,
but only one can be proved.
yet the majority of the world is convinced
that the other one is more true.

what kinda mindset is this,
where we rely on faith over facts
it's this type of thinking
that keeps us in lack.

lack of knowledge of self
lack of resources and wealth.

MO'REESE MADU

cuz we got more faith in jesus
than we do our own self.
we were such a powerful people
before we were introduced to religion.
we used to rely on mother nature
to guide us in all of our decisions.

and nature never failed us
because she is based on facts.
we didn't need to believe in her
cuz we could physically see her acts.

she gave us food and water
from the same dirt that birthed us.
she supplied all our needs
and her giving was surplus.

but we left her for religion
so now we have to rely on faith.
which leaves perpetually oppressed
relying on jesus to escape.

israelites & muslims

i got mad respect
for the hebrew israelites
and the nation of islam.
cuz they both took the
book of their oppressors
and revolutionized it to
give us some salaam.

the hebrew israelites
made me aware of our plight
and helped me to see
the bible with new eyes.
the nation of islam
inspired me from a distance
to do for myself no matter what,
even if that meant selling bean pies.

a lot of good comes
from them both
they take a lot out the hood
and give them hope
me, myself included,
before religion i was selling dope.

but despite all the good they've done
their foundations are still based on myths
you can see both of their original stories
on the ancient egyptian hieroglyphs.

what we have been given
are european & arabian
interpretations of african spirituality.
so for those of us who
practice these faiths,
it europeanizes & arabianizes our personality.

this is why we can't unite
and overcome oppression
cuz we think and act like the
same people causing our oppression.

these religions got us divided
over whose god is the best
condemning each other over
what's written in man-made texts.

tho our past black leaders who introduced us
to these religions had good intentions,
they both have now been infiltrated
by various government assistants.

UP FROM RELIGION

sure, both faiths have their pros
but they're outweighed by their cons
and the elite of the world use these
books to play us like pawns.

no disrespect to those who
practice them, i'm just stating the facts
the bible and the koran are good places to start
but at some point you gotta grow up from that.

post-traumatic slave syndrome

when it comes to my people,
a lot of our history is missing.
it was stolen during slavery,
to keep us in submission.

with no past to draw from,
we accepted the narratives that were given.
that we were pagan savages
that needed our sins forgiven.

blinded by the lies
of the europeans,
many denounced being
african or native caribbeans.

to make matters worse,
they taught us that black skin was a curse.
which caused us to hate ourselves
for something we couldn't reverse.

self-hate became the tool
to keep us enslaved.
by controlling our minds,
they could predict how we behaved.

because we hated ourselves
we hated on each other.
meanwhile treating our oppressor
as our brother.

this mindset was passed down
from generation to generation,
which is why so many black people today
still think like they on the plantation.

instead of fighting for freedom,
we fight against each other
yet are loving and kind
with white folks and others.

we don't know who we are,
so we treat each other like strangers.
the only time we unite is when
we are in some type of danger.

this type of behavior
will never get us free.
we must relearn who we are
if we want lib-er-ty.

negropeans

they took away our names
and gave us their names instead.
they prevented us from speaking our language
and made us speak their language instead.
they forbid us from practicing our spirituality
and taught us their religion instead.
they stripped us of our cultural traditions
and forced us to practice theirs instead.
they split our families up
and gave us their family instead.
they taught us that our skin and hair was ugly
and influenced us to look like them instead.
they trained us to hate each other
and to love them instead.
they told us that we were stupid,
and to be smart like them instead.
they told us we couldn't make it on our own,
and to depend on them instead.
they stole our true identity
and gave us theirs instead.

self-hate

we were once all
beautifully black as the night;
worshiped and adored by whites
for our melanated delight.

then they enslaved us, raped us;
and our skin started to become light.
polluting our dna with the same
recessive genes that makes them white.

fast forward to today,
we're all different shades of colors,
from dark brown to extremely bright.
and we're so mentally colonized and confused
that we hate our blackness
and prefer to look white.

marrying the daughters and sons of
the same folks who enslaved us;
thinking that it just might.
help us climb up the social ladder
of america by proudly having
mixed children that can pass for white.

now the same melanated beings
that were once worshiped for
being black and noble like knights
are now worshipping the
same whites that enslaved and
raped them; in hindsight.

i see black women's pain

as i walk through the valley
of the shadow of deception.
i see religion is also causing
my sister's depression.

indoctrinated to believe
that you are the daughters of eve
got you thinking you came from a man
and sent here to please all of his needs.

forced to sit in the back
told that only men can take the lead.
shuts down all of her dreams
and causes her soul to bleed.

she just wants to be useful
but nobody will give her the keys.
all they want her to do is take
care of the house, ya know, those sorts of things.

seeking for god to ease her pain,
keeps her praying on her knees.
not realizing she's a goddess and all life
comes forth in between those same knees.

she's often overlooked at home
at school and the church.
she longs for the day that someone
will recognize her worth.

not knowing her own value
she looks for it in others.
and she's often treated like a clearance sale
even by her own brothers.

she just wants to be loved
by a brother from her same race.
but everyone she's been with
keeps treating her with disgrace.

she crosses path with her
soulmate
from a previous lifetime.
but he ain't a christian or a muslim
so she's taught that he ain't the right kind.

her faith got her so spiritually blind
she's unable to access her inner divine.
so she shows off her body
to reveal what she can't find inside.

sending off the wrong vibrations
attracts many men who
want to skip the conversations
and get straight to having
sexual relations.
her body has needs
so she surrenders to the temptation.
but she always regrets it afterward,
resulting in a cycle of inner frustration.

tired of the abuse and
double standards of men.
she considers finding love
from another wo-man.

she finds companionship in a lady
who treats her like a queen.
but she's condemned by everyone
every time they hit the scene.

plus the relationship feels too unnatural,
so she just goes back to being single.
confused and hurt, she loses her
desire to even mingle.

the church says she's lost
and tells her to recommit to christ.
unaware of any other options,
she makes the alter call and surrenders her life.

she hides her tears inside
from falling down her face.
and goes to church every week
hoping one day god will fill her space.

my heart goes out to my sistas
stuck in this valley of deception.
i pray that your spirit awakens
and gives you a new perception.

cuz we need you.

you are queens
and the mothers
of all human things.
without your existence
there wouldn't be anything.

UP FROM RELIGION

stop looking outside yourself
for validation and love.
everything you seek
already lives within you,
not in the sky above.

i'm yo brotha
from anotha
giving you the game.
i just wanna see you win,
and be free from pain.

she is the messiah

forget what the bible say about
suffering not a woman to teach
and her not being useful outside
of being someone's helpmeet.

black women are goddesses
black women are queens
black women were the first
to birth human beings.

she's the life-giver. the nurturer.
the feminine power behind all great things.
she gives birth to all black men,
so we all got black women's genes.

her dna goes way back. hundreds of thousands
of years before adam and eve.
and out of her came hundreds of thousands
of the earth's most intelligent beings.

she is powerful beyond measure
and has the potential to create anything.
with her smile alone, she can inspire
a thug to become a king.

UP FROM RELIGION

she not only inspires greatness,
she is the personification of it.
who else you know can work a 9-5,
run a side business, go to school, and
still raise her own children and their cousins?

she does so much for others,
that she often neglects herself.
if her love was a currency,
she'd own all this nation's wealth.

ain't no woman like a sistah,
she got that sacred vibration.
from her spirit to her melanin
down to her presence and conversation.

she got that black girl magic.
when you meet her, you gotta have it.
i'm talkin' bout her love and companionship,
not just her body for you to smash it.

though her lovin is amazing
the soul beneath her flesh is even better.
hot enuff to make the coolest brothas
break down and have to sweat her.

but she's more than a mate
she's also a loyal friend.
the type to speak life into your soul
just cuz she wanna see you win.

that's why to know her is to love her,
whether you her husband, friend, son, or brother.
cuz what she brings to the table
can't be delivered by another.

black women are the best thing
that has ever happened to the planet.
she's so necessary to our survival
that we often take her for granted.

what would we do without our
sistahs, mothers, and wives?
just the thought of having to,
should bring tears to our eyes.

i love you black women.
and i hope the men in your circle do too.
cuz truth be told, none of us men
could have survived this long without you.

UP FROM RELIGION

after 400 years of oppression,
and no god or messiah coming to save us
from any of the books that they gave us.
it was the black woman and her ancestors
that kept us going and inspired to remain courageous.

so to me, the black woman is the messiah,
cuz she's the only redeemer that i know.
plus all hue-man life comes from her,
if you know of another, please let me know.

this poem is inspired by my mom, grandma and wife,
the three most important black women in my life.
sometimes i wish i could go back in time
to experience yall's love twice.

black accountability for white supremacy

i used to think that we were
just victims of white supremacy.
until i researched the history
of this systematic conspiracy.
and then slowly but surely
it became crystal clear to me.
that we are also the biggest
supporters of white supremacy.

we degrade our own women
let our oppressors raise our children.
go to church and worship a white god
to numb all the pain that feeling.
and then celebrate the murder and rape
of our ancestors for thanksgiving.
i know it sounds crazy and ignant
but this is really how we livin.
supporting our own demise
and indoctrinating our children.
teaching our sons to wait on jesus
while 64,000 of our daughters are missing.

no wonder the youth no longer take adults serious
the shit we out here doing is just straight-up ridiculous.

UP FROM RELIGION

we either stay broke due to giving
10% of all our income to religion.
or we end up selling our souls
chasing the bag for fractions of a million.
spending all our money on brands
that make white folks a killin.
marrying the oppressor's daughter
passing our wealth down to their children.
how can we expect to overcome oppression
by making these types of decisions?
we have become our own worst enemy
and are in dire need of healing.

we don't support our true leaders
until they are dead.
we don't accept esoteric knowledge
unless it comes from what some white man said.
we don't teach our children
they learn from european institutions instead.
we don't start our own communities
integrating with others is widespread.

we spend our money with strangers
rather than with our own people.
then complain about the unemployment rates
and wages not being equal.

we shoot and kill each other
but respond to those who kill us with being peaceful.
and wonder why generation after generation
we keep reaping the same sequel.

how long we gon keep marching and voting for change
our own children mock us; like damn my parents deranged.

we need to return back to us
cuz we the only ones we can trust.
but we've been so tainted with the lust
of what america has to offer us.
that we perpetually chase integration
rather than just taking care of us.
then blame white supremacy as a crutch
for why we remain economically in the dust.
avoiding taking responsibility of the reality
that nobody is defeating us, except us.

still slaves

in order to overcome oppression,
we must decolonize our minds.
way too many of us
still have the white man's mind.

they took away our names
and we never gave them back.
therefore we still belong to the slavemaster
that owned us from way back.

the dream of the oppressed
is to become like their oppressor.
so whenever black folks get some power,
we usually end up oppressing each other.

we claim we want freedom,
yet we crucify those tryin to lead us off the plantation.
cuz truth be told, many of us prefer to have
a seat at the master's table over having liberation.

colorism

light skin, dark skin,
black skin, brown skin.
we come in all different shades
of the same ancient melanin.

the darkest is the oldest,
and the lightest is the newest,
but no matter which shade we're clothed in,
we are humanity's truest.

so don't get caught
up into colors and shades.
that's a divisive tactic
from the willie lynch days.

whatever your melanin is,
it's a gift from god.
don't let anyone make you
feel excluded or odd.

black is beautiful
and so is beige and brown.
you are royalty, clothed
in a melanin crown.

royalty

we are a
royal priesthood
from ancient african *nations*.
we migrated all
over the planet and
established the first *civilizations*.

from asia
to australia,
from spain to the *americas*.
we were the first
people to manifest
each continent's *esoterica*.

we have been the
light of the world for
thousands of *years*.
and we continue to
shine despite all of the
oppression and *tears*.

nobody could do
this but us; that's why
everybody wanna be just *like us*.

we influenced the entire
world; yet they give the
credit to everyone *but us.*

our black magic
is so powerful; we got
enough to share until *infinity.*
but we will never
overcome oppression
until we recognize our *divinity.*

we are our ancestors'
children; descendants
of royal *stars.*
as mufasa told simba
we just need to remember
who we *are.*

we came before columbus

blacks were the first in america
so this land belongs to us.
many of our ancestors came here from africa
way before columbus, so we are indi-gen-ous.

we cultivated these lands
and lived in harmony with nature.
we traded our resources with our brothers in africa
who were known as master sailors.

we ruled the americas
thousands of years before the arrival
of mongolians and europeans.
we had established civilizations
from north america to the caribbeans.

but then the catholic church used
christianity to enslave blacks and
take over their lands.
christopher columbus and other
colonizers was sent here
to carry out their plan.

we fought back
for hundreds of years
until christianity took over our minds
and subdued us into fears.
which led to us losing our lands
known historically as the trail of tears.

some of the indians also enslaved us
and helped the white man take over our estates.
then they assumed our true identities and
became known as the natives of the states.

with so many allies against us
we were never able to recoup.
so we chose to fight for our freedom
by becoming part of the u.s. troops.

that still didn't gain us freedom
so we joined the government
to fight for our civil rights.
but our leaders fell in love with money
and our freedom left their sights.

UP FROM RELIGION

we slowly gave up our black power
to be integrated with whites.
now we apart of the same
system that's causing our plight.

voting for democrats and republicans
hoping they will keep their word.
ignoring the fact that they are
two wings apart of the same bird.

but we don't need a civil rights,
we just need the spirit to fight.
for the land of our birthrights
so we end our 400 year plight.

we are gods among men
and just like africa, the americas is our land.
so if we're gonna remain here,
then we should reclaim our brand.

ancestor homage

they like to call our ancestors slaves.
as if they were genetically born in chains.

but slaves aren't born, slaves are made.

made by being socialized
to think and act like your oppressor.
and raised in a system
that has always treated you as lesser.

growing up in environments like this,
causes you to seek to be like those who hate you.
but in mimicking them, you internalize their ways
and end up hating you too.

then you have children and
pass your self-hatred on to them.
and they also grow up desiring
to be like those who don't look like them.

the cycle continues
for generation after generation.
this is why so many of us today
still have mindsets of slaves on the plantation.

not because we were born like this,
but because we were made into this.
and the only way out of this
is to remember who we were
before we were made into this.

niggas didn't come from africa
niggas were made in america.
royal nations came from africa
that's how we built up america.

our ancestors' free labor
made us the world power.
that's why they hate us so much
cuz they recognize our power.

they study ways to keep us divided
through secret agencies like the c.i.a.
cuz they know like kendrick lamar,
that we got royalty in our dna.

religion was the number one tool
used to disconnect us from our genetic genius.
they convinced us to replace our african deities
of power with a man named jesus.

now we subconsciously look
at white people as the image of god.
so we try to imitate them
to be more like god.

this prevents us from
reconnecting to our roots,
which keeps us in a perpetual cycle
of reaping bad fruits.

if only we knew,
we could tap back into our source,
the source of our ancestors
that lives within us.

though their bodies perished,
their spirit still lives
and they're here to help us
navigate throughout our years.

but we too caught up in religion
to receive their guidance
so the ancestors' power living within us
just remains silent.

UP FROM RELIGION

yet they still try to contact us
by speaking to our minds and spirit.
but religion has made us so spiritually deaf,
that we can't even hear it.

so when we have dreams or hear voices,
we credit it to jesus or god.
not even knowing or considering,
those are our ancestors living spiritually abroad.

some from ancient times,
some from our recent family lines.
just trying to connect with us,
and make sure everything is fine.

the power is in our ancestors,
because they are our source.
and once we return back to honoring them,
we will get back on course.

come out of her my people

after 400 plus years,
america still shows us no *respect*.
yet we continue to march, *protest*
get violent and *upset*.
like these people gonna change
and make things *correct*.
but that ain't never gone happen,
at least i'm willing to *bet*.
because as w.e.b dubois said, "a system
cannot fail those it was never created to *protect*."

the constitution was created to
make white supremacy *legal*.
and it hasn't been updated
cuz they still believe that this philosophy is *regal*.
their myth of white being pure
but black is *evil*.
is why the court system still doesn't
treat blacks and whites as *equal*.

we need to stop trying to integrate into their *system*
to be *one with them*.
cuz it makes us take on their mind
and *become like them*.

seeking money and power
at the expense of those they see as *less than them*.
got us birthing crabs in a barrel fighting to
make the next brother or sista *sink than swim*.
this type of behavior
keeps us *oppressed by them*
and like sista assata shakur told us, "nobody
in history has ever gotten their freedom by appealing
to the moral sense of the people *oppressing them*."

so how bout we unplug from their matrix
and start our own governmental *rules*.
take back control over our lands
and reformat our ancestral tribal *crews*.
maybe move to the tropics or Africa
and relearn nature's *rules*.
then rebuild up our nations that
was stolen by the arabs and *jews*.
we tried everything else,
so what have we got to *lose*?
ain't no need to keep complaining
and singing america's *blues*.
if we really want freedom,
then we have to pay our *dues*.
cuz if we keep playing the system's game,
we will continue to *lose*.

CHAPTER FOUR

the lessons

do you

if your religion makes you a
better person, then i'm all for it.
but if it does the opposite,
then you need to ignore it.

don't pretend that god is good
if he really hasn't been.
being true to yourself might hurt
but it ain't no sin.

follow your heart,
and trust wherever it leads you.
plus be willing to let go of
anything that depletes you.

we all got flaws,
whether we realize it or not.
and we all have good in us,
whether we religious or not.

so do you and be you
and allow others to do and be them too.
cuz you can never tell on the surface
what people be going through.

be light

don't condemn those
in darkness for not being
who you want them to be.
just be a light to them
so they can see
what you see.

no amount of
condemnation will end
the darkness of night.
only love and
inspiration can bring
forth the light.

you can't force people
to change. you can only
inspire them to.
if they look at your
life, what will it
inspire them to do?

compassion

never come to
final conclusions
about a person's way.
just as you are
a continual work in
progress, so are they.

always give people
the same grace
for their journey
as you would like
others to give you
for your journey.

just because the path that you
are on is right for you.
doesn't mean that it's the right
path for others too.

mercy is only
given to the merciful.
we all make mistakes
so deal with people versatile.

g-code

respect everybody's beliefs;
whether it comes from
the bible, the koran or the torah.
how you treat folks that
think different from you
tells a lot about your aura.

ain't none of us holy,
we just doing the best we can
with the knowledge we've been given.
plus we all on different paths,
so what matters the most
is how you live it.

you ain't gotta
be a priest to
have morals.
your actions just gotta
line up with what comes
out your orals.

tribalizms

everybody of
yo complexion
ain't headed in
yo same direction.

sometimes you have to love
your kinfolk from a distance
so they don't put you off course
from fulfilling your life's mission.

don't follow anyone
who says they are color blind.
they're just making excuses
to avoid society's color lines.

be good to all races
but put no group before your own.
without a social code of ethics
you will have no people to call home.

let go

forgive yourself
for leading people astray.
you gotta bigger purpose
move yo ego out the way.

take off the mask
you wear to hide your pains,
it's wearing you out and
giving you no gains.

no need to be ashamed
we all make mistakes.
but never let your errors
stop you from becoming great.

when things aren't adding up in your life,
that's a sign it's time to start subtracting.
you only get one life to live in this flesh
so choose truth over satisfaction.

wholeness

i forgot
how love felt.
until i learned to be still
to listen and to feel
the vibration of god
flowing within myself.

feeling the frequency
of my soul's essence.
allowed me to
experience
love through
participating
in manifesting
its message.

know thyself

i spent so much time trying
to please a god i couldn't see.
that i didn't notice the one
in the mirror looking back at me.

when i stopped looking
for a god to save me from my sins.
i realized that i was my own savior
i just needed to go within.

once i lost my religion,
i began to find myself.
now life is more fulfilling
because i finally know myself.

i am the heartbeat of
the most high's vibration.
my life is a visual frequency
of my inner conversations.

know thy ancestors

they told us not to call on our ancestors
because it was evil and pagan.
yet the church is always calling
on abraham, isaac, and jacob.

they want us to pray to a dead white man
that never shows up to answer our prayers,
rather than praying to our ancestor spirits
who are always right there.

if god had to go through
our ancestors to bring us forth.
then shouldn't we have to go through
our ancestors to connect to source?

the enemy within

the devil only exists
to those who believe in him
so if you want him to disappear from
your life, then just stop believing in him.
ain't nobody coming to
torment us after we die
we're already tormenting the hell out
of our ourselves believing in this lie.

the real enemy lives within
our mental illness is our greatest sin
if we can just overcome ourselves
then we are guaranteed to win.

you are the one

until you realize
that you are
the god of
yourself

you will always
be dependent on
something outside
yourself.

...

you are god
in the flesh
hidden in
melanin's best

remember who
you are and
don't settle
for less.

inner voice

that burning
desire you feel on the
inside of your heart's core

is your higher self
telling you to level up
and become more.

...

become who your
spirit is calling
you to be

not who mainstream
society is programming
you to be.

discernment

the job of the
oppressor is to enslave you,
not save you

so don't expect to
find salvation from reading
a book that he gave you.

…

when your god
and your savior come from
your oppressor and enslaver.

it dictates
your behavior
to act in their favor.

earth school

the earth is a classroom
for the lessons that our souls
didn't learn in the past incarnation.
yet when we come back to life
we get so caught up in this flesh
that we lose our concentration.

earth is hell
and the spirit realms
are the heavens.
but we can't ascend to spirit
until the flesh
learns its lessons.

we're all on different levels
in the earth school of life.
bounded by this flesh
until our soul becomes a light.
so don't judge people over pettiness
just try to understand their plight.

CHAPTER FIVE

the affirmations

black love

love your people
as you love yourself.
after all, we're all
we got left.

uplift yourself
so you can uplift others as well
instead of hating and fighting
let's be each other's help.

we are one blood; so how we see
each other is how we see our self,
tho we have many different stories
our book comes from the same shelf.

let love lead in all our interactions
so that the cold hearts can melt
and we can vibe on the same frequency
until a global healing is felt.

unity

seek to understand others,
before you seek to be understood.
your knowledge is worthless
if your heart is no good.

the leaders who get
the most out of people
are the ones who care
the most about their people.

selfishness makes us
enemies to each other
but selflessness unites us
with each other.

the fastest way to succeed
is by helping others succeed.
we each have what
the other needs.

forgiveness

hold no offenses
in your heart.
they may drive-in but
don't give them a place to park.

be quick to admit your wrongs
and make amends.
you never know when you won't
see that person again.

forgive yourself
we all miss some steps.
ain't no blueprint to life
we learn and grow, each step.

vibrations

give the type of love
that you desire to receive.
your vibration will send you
the harvest of your seed.

be the attitude that
you want to be around.
your vibration will attract
those with a like sound.

act like
your potential.
your vibration will
make it sequential.

inward power

your life flows
in whatever direction
your mind goes.

the habitual self-talk that
goes on in our heads
manifest itself outwardly
showing us what's been said.

consciousness
is the only reality.
our circumstances are formed
by our true personality.

once you fix
what's wrong within
a new reality
will begin.

submit to spirit

your spirit remembers the plan
you made for this lifetime.
become one with your divinity
so you can fulfill your mission this time.

sometimes you have to starve
the flesh to feed the spirit.
so when the source speaks,
you not too full to hear it.

be still and know
that you are god.
listen to your spirit
and salute it with a nod.

spirituality you're born with,
it's religion you're taught.
know your worth.
so you can never be bought.

courage

research all
received information.
that is the only
true education.

if you close
your eyes to facts.
darkness will be on
everything you attract.

seek for truth
in all you do.
and your well-being
will steadily accrue.

walk yo path

live oblivious to
the tune of public opinion.
what people think of you
is none of your business.

never surrender your convictions
to make other people feel secure.
stay true to who you are and those
who are for you will endure.

once the fear in you dies
you will then become alive.
and the best part of you
will no longer be hidden inside.

futuristic

don't let
your history
stop you from
reaching your destiny.

turn the page and
let a new life happen to you.
the past was just your class
for what's about to happen to you.

get out of your way
and make room for new visions.
don't be led astray
by your past decisions.

you are the
master of your life
it's time to stop stalling
and become a KRIST.

lol

laugh when life
gets too serious
it will keep you
from going delirious.

guard those around you
who make you smile
they make life seem
more worthwhile.

a good joke
will cure any pain
so think of sumn funny
when you feelin insane.

the joy of laughter
regenerates the soul
it keeps your essence young
as your body grows old.

observations

religion ain't the way
nature is the cure.

technology is okay
but it's just an allure.

what we call time
is really just a blur.

we living in the matrix,
that's for sure.

reality

the weak create excuses,
the strong create solutions.

the religious bring division.
the spiritualists give you vision.

the artists make you think.
the system keeps you asleep.

the truth sets you free.
the lies enslave you to thee.

woke

i can do all things through
my ancestors who strengthen me
those who were once flesh and blood
are still manifesting spiritually.

no religion necessary
to accomplish the extraordinary.
what's decoded in my d-n-a
sends me messages like a secretary.

tho the pressure to reach my
potential can sometimes be weary.
i can't let my ancestors down,
i'm too proud of the torch that i carry.

plus my soul so old
that i'm already legendary.
so i ain't gotta be famous,
my words is revolutionary.

self-love

this year i turned 32.
i can't believe all that
i have grown through.

so much has changed
so much wisdom gained.
i would be a fool to remain the same.

the veil has been removed
and i can now see-through.
both the lies and the truth.
no longer bound by the
indoctrination from my youth.

on a lifelong journey of healing
and becoming my best self.
learning something new everyday
cause my knowledge is my wealth.

ain't perfect, still rough
around the edges.
but i'm a man of integrity
willing to change, like sketches.

not for you,
but for me.
spent years pleasing others,
now i'm doing what's best for me.

eyes wide open,
woke as i ever been.
comfortable standing out,
not looking to fit in.

i'm in love. with myself.
my wife. my children. and my people.
looking forward to what's ahead
stay tuned for my sequel.

Index

ain't no hell, 84
ancestor homage, 114
back to church, 7
be light, 123
biblical oppression, 46
black accountability for white supremacy, 104
black love, 138
church boy, 2
colorism, 108
come out of her my people, 118
compassion, 124
courage, 144
discernment, 134
do you, 122
dope boy, 4
earth school, 135
every 7 years, 42
evolution, 68
facts vs. faith, 85
following the followers, 16
for my little ones, 74
forgive me queens, 37
forgiveness, 140
freedom, 64
futuristic, 146
g-code, 125
god ain't good, 51
humbled, 62
i see black women's pain, 95
i thought we were israelites, 11
inner voice, 133
inward power, 142
israelites & muslims, 87
know thy ancestors, 130
know thyself, 129
kush therapy, 66
let go, 127
little god, 130
locked up by religion, 9
lol, 147
lost is the way, 59
mind control, 82

my way out, 61
native american roots, 71
negropeans, 92
no mo, 63
observations, 148
ode to malcolm x, 76
ode to moms & pops, 30
on my own: true story, 20
post traumatic slave syndrome, 90
purpose, 78
r.i.p. cliff, 39
reality, 149
revelations, 60
royalty, 109
salute to wifey, 34
self-hate, 93
self-love, 151
self-righteous, 54
she is the messiah, 100
still slaves, 107
submit to spirit, 143
the enemy within, 131
the jesus myth, 48
torah blues, 14
tribalizms, 126
unity, 139
up from religion, 28
vibrations, 141
walk yo path, 145
we came before columbus, 111
who is god?, 57
wholeness, 128
woke, 150
you are the one, 132

Acknowledgements

Up From Religion could not have been written without the loving support of my wife, Ashley. A book in progress for me is like having a new child – it's heartwarming but very demanding and requires almost all your time. Having her by my side, not only helped me complete this poetry collection but also was the inspiration behind some of its content. So, I am very grateful to have her as my partner in this journey called life.

About The Author

Maurice Lindsay is an author, screenwriter, and entrepreneur. He was previously known for the blog, TruthOverTradition.com, in which he published over one hundred articles between the years of 2012 and 2019 to an international readership of primarily the African Diaspora. *Up From Religion* is his debut collection of poetry. Maurice currently lives in Columbia, South Carolina with his wife and children. You can connect with him online at AfrovisionsMedia.com.

www.ingramcontent.com/pod-product-compliance
Lightning Source LLC
Chambersburg PA
CBHW020416080526
44584CB00014B/1358